Other Books by Moyra Donaldson

Kissing Ghosts (1995)
Beneath the Ice (2001)

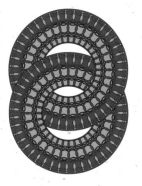

SNA

SNAKESKIN
STILETTOS

Moyra Donaldson

CavanKerry ❖ Press Ltd.

Library of Congress Cataloging-in-Publication Data

Donaldson, Moyra.
   Snakeskin stilettos / by Moyra Donaldson.
       p. cm.
   ISBN 0-9707186-0-8
   1. Northern Ireland–Poetry.   I. Title.
PR6054.04597 S63 2001
821'.914–dc2   2001042503

Some of the poems in this book appeared in
*Poetry Ireland Review, The H.U. Gown Literary Supplement, Women's
Works, Sunday Tribune Magazine, The Independent* (London), and
Cimarron Review, or were broadcast on BBC Radio Ulster.

Previously published by Lagan Press, Belfast,
Northern Ireland

Cover and text design by Random Features Industries

First edition

CavanKerry Press Ltd.
Fort Lee, New Jersey
www.cavankerrypress.com

Jack and Nessa

CONTENTS

Foreword

by Medbh McGuckian

It is a rare pleasure to come across a poetry that is a source of simple enjoyment, that ultimately does not depress. Moyra's is uniquely valuable in a social as well as a literary sense, charting as it so subtly does the emergence of a delightful, sensitive, all-embracing personality from a repressive religious environment in which "his word was law." If the politicians and streetfighters of Northern Ireland could learn the lessons she teaches here, if the readers in America could appreciate them, a new climate of understanding would blossom.

Her determination is to explore the realities, but also the limits and beyond, of living itself; then of living peculiarly as a married woman in "soft Ulster evenings" with their tensions, of trying as such a constrained woman to live spiritually in an all-Ireland poetic context, and thus absorb lateish in life those rich pagan influences from land, sea, star and mountains that Mary O'Malley, for example, born and bred in Galway, was lucky enough to imbibe with her mother's milk.

These poems abound in narratives, observations, drama scenery, character, speech, colour, atmosphere. Like nothing so much as the plays of Synge, you are there with the people, whether it be at a hospital bedside, in a marital or lovers' bed, on a skirmish through memory, taking a holiday excursion. Place is created as carefully as season is evoked, from India Street in Belfast to Newgrange and Mayo; from Athens to Liverpool. She locates her imagination and fires it while pinning it down. Mythic personal names such as Leda, Rapunzel, Kali, which are an element Nuala ní Dhomhnaill is expert in swimming in, drift alongside actual names from our present world, and the borders between shift constantly under her control.

The most attractive, never mind seductive, quality of this first collection is its honesty, a convincing intimacy of tone, rewarding us with the sense that we are being offered the truth and given a key to some of the most secret rooms of a heart. That recurrent word ''skin'' and ruminations on the self, its transmutations, its unities with others, its dissolving capacities, reminds me of no less a mentality than Yeats'—with an extra dash of daring and sensuality.

I dare myself to hope that American readers will find her charming, disarming, open, warm, even tender by turn, but also sharp as an apple in a fairytale. In whatever guise she appears, from dream to dream, her revelations are as instructive, wisely flowing, rhythmic and appetizing as a pair of sexy shoes you are just dying to put on.

What ground is mine
if I would govern myself?
Where is my country
if neither bogs nor gantries
speak of me?
Where can I stand
if I am not one thing,
or the other?

EXILE

My grandfather knew where he stood.
Ancestors planted his feet
in fertile soil, green futures were
named in his name, possessed.
He preached their flinty faith
in mission tents, visions of eternal life
on soft Ulster evenings,

but there was no redemption.
Not in the land, or through the Blood.
Not in the hard lessons of duty, obedience,
with which he marked his children.

He is stripped of virtue,
his legacy a stone
of no magic, no transcendence.
No children ever turn to swans,
wafer remains wafer on the tongue,
and flesh is always flesh.

My two white birds will bring me
water from the mountains,
beakfuls of sweet sips.
I will grow a new tongue,
paint my body with circles
and symbols of strength, mark myself
as one who belongs in the desert.

ASTRONOMY

Like Gulliver, I lie immobilised, but yet
content to let the moss grow on my limbs and sides.
Tendrils of ferns unfurl before and through my eyes,
my head is full of buds—so though I do regret
the loss of much—here in this place so much remains.
Besides, freedom is treacherous, for even when
you tread with care, not trusting eyes to know for sure
what's solid ground, or what's just air: your heart retains
the memory of the sudden drop, the letting down.
Now I'm so still that small birds make their nests in me.
I watch the stars move in their paths above my head:
almost content. So far below, and closely bound.

THINKING
ABOUT
AUTUMN

I was looking at the garden
and thinking about autumn
and how I just can't like it
despite the colours of leaves
dahlias fat ripe elderberries
blackberries hips and haws
because it means winter's coming
and I don't like winter
despite how snow looks
on the trees I can see
from my kitchen window
frosty night stars
big fires and hot whiskeys
then I thought maybe I
should just learn
to content myself
because after all
it's the nature of things
and after winter there is
always spring and I love spring
the way may blossom is unbelievably
white and everything is bursting out
growing reaching moving
into lovely lovely summer
sun and bare skin
long light and short hot nights
then I saw the birds
lined up on the telephone lines
ready for leaving and I thought
screw contentment
if I had wings I'd go too.

MOTHER WHO HAS BEEN

my broken bowl   my holy grail

my long silence   my spoken truth

my tiny bound feet   my seven league boots

my never quite   my every first prize

when you come on the forgotten well among the trees,
lower the bucket, hand over hand: the rope will hold
as you draw up the cold clear water. Feel how it cools
your blood's wild fire, scorched earth greens back, seeds burst,
and you can read again the hieroglyphics of branches,
budding across the sky. Birds wake to fly and small animals
uncurl among the nascent ferns. Listen—
a child's untroubled voice rings on the morning air, singing
as you fetch water for your mother from the wood well

and nothing will be lost.
Here is your father, once the youngest boy
neighbours had ever seen between
the handles of a plough, the hardest worker.
He lies under my heart carved in stone,
grown to the man who never wept.
Soft as a breast, your mother
is my children's remembered dream of milky mouths.
Each thought undone, each memory unpeeled,
each year of you, I fold, hold to my cheek
like the white linen your grandmother sewed
by candlelight. I breathe you in, the living skin of me
knowing it was always too late for us, for everything
happens as it must, in its own moment.

As I become the past on which the future rests,
forgiveness is a final irrelevance.
Years from now, on some perfect summer evening,
I will look and you'll be in the garden, gathering fruit.
A small dog will follow at your heels

as you pick gooseberries, bursting juice,
strawberries, red ripe under leaves.
When you see me, you will beckon me to come,
and I'll run down the years into your arms.

VISITS

She's quite content today,
chatting with Margaret and Meta,
but I am struggling.
What does it signify,
their conversation?
A raggle of crows
blown sideways in an east wind
across a flat canvas, a flat sky,
a world without horizons.
In this new landscape,
I am still the outsider,
the only one who thinks it matters—
perspective, the earth's curve.

She wants to go home,
to where her mother is waiting
by the first shining hearth.
She wants to go home
as a child can ache
for love forever.

She knows I'm not a stranger,
the family face familiar still:
a sister perhaps?
I crouch, dreaming
behind a latticework of words—
red lips, blood
spilling from a bowl,
dark stains of unconsciousness.

She moves away from me
down the corridor,
just a strange old woman
scuttling along,
bent on her own business,
nothing to do with me at all.

12:05 AM NEW YEAR'S DAY

Church bells chime the change,
and the new is rung in.
As the ground glitters with frost
so does the sky with stars,
and I am standing somewhere in-between
guessing at constellations,
trying to sense the ancient imagination
that saw and named them.
I hear your voice, reciting the catechism,
questions and answers.
I close my eyes and see the nebulae
of blood vessels, the galaxies of nerves,
the imploded shadows inside your head;
black holes down which you flow
as space and time distorts.
I watch but cannot follow,
and you are almost out of sight already,
approaching the singularity,
moving beyond answers.

WHAT
SHE
MIGHT
PRAY

No matter how far I have drifted,
even if land is nowhere to be seen,
do not let the sea completely own me.
I could not bear to hear no other rhythm
but the tide's relentlessness.
Do not abandon me. Anchor me with love.

WATCHER

When there is nothing left but shadow,
I will sit with you
under the December evening sky,
under its red and black disintegration,
until even the mountains, cutting
their perfect shapes across our horizon,
are subsumed into night.

RIPPLES

She says
his word was law.
If he'd said–there's a blue tree–
we wouldn't even have looked,
we'd have known the tree was blue.

She cries
a child's pain from an old woman's mouth,
and I am listening to generations of myself.

SIDE WARD

Wrapped up neatly in the past tense
by busy nieces and their families,
I wait. My nights have become endless.
Footsteps in the corridor, machinery's hum,
my fingers rustling like paper on the sheets.
Mornings have shrunk to a medicinal routine.
The thermometer, placed between my dry lips,
blood pressure, catheter checked.
Needles pushed beneath translucent skin.
I try to remember when my body
was a private thing–closed.
Spiralling in and out of thinnest sleep,
the pictures come; scenes and faces
from the past, hanging in air.
What was, what might have been.
Fact, impression, dream?
The difference hardly seems to matter anymore.
No one remains to hear the telling of my years,
like beads unstrung they scatter, roll away.
This odour of decay I smell on my own breath
repels all visitors, except the ghosts–
and only nurses hold my hand, or call me love.

MUSE

she is
little bird
tiger
hoarder
storyteller
wisewoman
fool

she has
made the past no place
but substance of her flesh
flesh of my dreams

HIBERNATING

Store what you may need again,
bonfire the worn out, the outgrown,
then slow—mid-winter's rhythm.
Enter a dreamless time,
and delta wave deep,
sleep out the past.

Do not wake
until the sun across your eyelids
promises a world of light.

A MODEST GHOST

My father is a modest ghost, undramatic,
not given to walking the long night watches,
or taking up a chair at family parties.
Rather, he appears from the spaces
between things, connections made,
inconspicuous moments tumbling
into consciousness as if by accident.
I have glimpsed his reflection in the
iridescent feathers of a pheasant,
startled in the early morning fields,
gone as soon as look.
A perfect note, held to breath's end
is the touch of his hand.

He's pleased I notice him, and understand.

B A B E
I N
T H E
W O O D S

Each time you abandoned me, daddy,
I followed the trail back home
until I was left with nothing but crumbs.
Half of me missing, phantom.

I did not want to be lost in the dark forest,
tangled in the hair of the skinny old witch
who eats children, feeds them sweet things,
then picks at their innocence with fingers of bone.

By the time you came looking for me
I was all gone, daddy. Licked up, swallowed down.

POEM
FOR
FOUR
CHILDREN

*

If I climb high enough, to where the ice never melts,
I believe I will find you,
a small girl, frozen for ever in supplication.
I will take you in my arms,
and pray for your sweet warm flesh, carry you
back to yourself.

*

My little tiger with centuries on your shoulder,
you are eating me up.
Come out of the dark stripe of jungle
so I can see you.
Forget the savage river that sometimes is
and sometimes is not
and curl yourself around me as if only I am home.
Let me stroke your beautiful head.

*

I remember you in the gap between seconds,
in the time beneath time,
in the future that was not, in the dream of I am.

*

Soon there will be no possibility of this child
that I have named in absence: Jack,
for fathers and grandfathers.
Already he is fading, like an old family photograph,
ghosts in his eyes.

SNAKESKIN STILETTOS

Eight years old, you understand
these shoes are different.
Not for nothing
has your mother wrapped them in paper,
shut them into their box, set them
at the very back of the wardrobe.
Forbidden.

You imagine them—
on their own in the dark,
hissing softly.
Biding their time.

Sneak in, creak open the door,
lift the lid and let them out,
untissue the fear.
Run your fingers
against the fissley scales,
press the fangs of heels
into your palm.
Something
you've never felt before.
These shoes are live and dangerous.

17

MY
TURN
TO
BE
THE
HORSE

for Jannah

I paw the tarmac,
snort long plumes of breath,
rejoicing in the strength
that flows along my back.
Muscle on bone
my strong straight limbs.
Sound joyful, rolls from belly
to trumpet-nostrils, trembling air.
Then rider taps a signal—go—and I

am
    rhythm
        running
            no walls stop
leap
    higher
       wider
         in to air
hooves
    crack earth
        spark stars
           blood gallops

loose. The bell rings, calling us again
to be corralled, and we trot into line.
Horse and rider tamed by long division,
comprehension, back to little girls.
Under the desk my hooves dissolve.

CHANGES

In mad March, nights with a blood moon,
I slip into the skin of a hare,
to run the fields, leap at the sky—
out from the pressed earth that holds my form.

When opiate summer drugs the nights,
my skin is a snake's, coiled
around the cool centre of knowing.
I hold serpent secrets, my eyes are planets.

I am never afraid in the thick hide of bear,
dipping my paws in icy rivers
to scoop and eat silver-quick swimming life.
All winter my belly is full, my sleep deep.

KALI

I am bound to returns, always
circling back to contain myself.
I deny your linear transcendence,
need nothing to make me complete.
I am a dark pool held by the moon,
yoked to rhythms inflexible, indifferent.
I am garden and serpent, walled, occult,
nature's impervious confederate.
I am a red maw, blind cave belly,
where all knowing must cease.
Your art is to define me smaller,
shutting me in to shut me out.

LEDA

All night she dreamt swan.
Warm rush of wings, cool beak on skin.
It did not occur to her to wonder
as she rose in a coupling of flight to bone,
throat on soft throat, speaking
the language of birds.

Only in the morning,
brushing down from her hair,
did she consider the event strange.

RAVEN

I foresee this moment:

I am lifted out of the Ark's dark belly, into the light.

Released from the tight cup of her hands, flight fills me
again.

I will owe nothing.

DREAM
AFTER
NEWGRANGE

I

Needing a break
they took a long weekend,
caught the sun
on a beach in the south.
The first real warmth
in a cold late spring,
winds from the north.
It lifted them,
gave them back appetite
so that they slept close,
woke early to the singing of birds.
Driving home again
they stopped at Newgrange,
bought ice-cream
and joined a queue to see inside.

Plunged into darkness
at the stone centre,
she reached for his hand,
held it tight,
but had no sense of him,
or of herself.
Lost in the absolute
absence of light.

II

At dawn her flesh sings
under his palm.
She is a bird, dreaming
in deep green forests
where mysteries need no solutions.
Light is a fine, precious beam
and she is feathered with praise.

LUST

Bearded old satyr,
the wind from the hills
is thick with your scent,
musty yet fresh,
a confusion of seasons.

Comfortable in the house of Pentheus,
with its fitted concepts,
its rational doors, leading always
from one place to the next,
she forgot you—became only human.

Then you rear again at her window,
swirled in your own myth.
Lines from an ancient script
calling her out into the hills,
where coiled snakes will lick her face
in the back seat of a parked car.

VAMPIRESS

No mortal dreams remain.
Thirst wakens me
to a narrow darkness,
night black against
my sin white skin.
The scent of your blood
is musk—like love.
My appetite is infinitely keen.

Come to the window,
let me in, I am your own
come back for you.
Don't be afraid my sweet,
to feel my little sharp teeth
against your skin.

POEM FOUND IN A CASTLE

Summer, when the hounds skulk
in buttress shadows, their tongues lolling,
this room remains damp, chill.
Its stone holds twelve months winter,
and forty winters have folded over me
in this ancestral place, where faith
is rock on rock, piled to the sky.
My husband led me to this chamber,
and I was cold despite the fire's burning.
He placed a torc of silver on my neck,
called me his wife: but I dreamt of my sisters,
woke as ice, in stone-grey castle air.

From the window I see my dark-haired sons
ride out with their father to hunt wild things,
they don't look back, but know I stand here
framed in stone: their cold and foreign mother.
I dream I am the falcon on his wrist, hooded,
I see no place to land, but back to him.

THE
IRISH
DERVISH

After the poteen had been passed round,
Tona–beatified–closed his eyes,
bare-knuckled the beat until blood flew
from his fingers: anointing us.
Hammered by live bones, the bodhran's skin
sang raw and red: thrilling, speeding
settled rhythms of heart and mind.
Spirits possessed us, held us
to a strange bliss, while the room
span–faster and faster–
about the centre where he stood.

SNOW WHITE

One bite
and it was as if I were dead.
You anointed me, dressed me in finery,
and laid me in my crystal box.
You placed beside me the few artefacts of my life,
then closed the lid and weeping all the while
shouldered my small weight to a clearing in the forest.
You left me there.
All this was done according to tradition.
Left to myself,
deer grazed at my feet, and on winter nights
the moon shone full in my face.
I saw seasons as ebb and flow of light
and knew myself as many things,
a vixen's footprint in new snow,
the delicate breast bone of a dove,
a stone held in a child's hand,
the apple in my own throat,
the kiss ...

RAPUNZEL

... a dead person,
coffin shaped,
her long hair
draped,
her hands crossed
over her belly,
her heels together.
Inside the dead cell
of her head,
a woman is trapped.
There is a window
but no door, no bars
on the window because
of the impossibly long way
down to the ground.
She rattles round
inside the bone,
alone and hearing
nothing but echoes until
she imagines terrible things—
she is a dead person ...

SONG FOR BONES

Listen—

there once was and was not, a seal woman
who seal swam, woman danced, both magnificent.
The man who saw her dancing on the rocks
by the moon's light, felt the great weight
of his loneliness lift from his chest.
In a moment, he had stolen her sealskin
from the rock where she'd left it.

When seal woman had danced to her heart's content,
she began to look for her sealskin
so that she could slip into the sea again.
More and more frantic, high and low, until
the man stepped forward. 'Woman, be my wife,'
he said. 'In seven summers I will return your sealskin
then you can go or stay as you please.'

Seal woman looked into his eyes for a long time and said,
'I will go with you and in seven summers it will be decided.'

In the second year a child was born, a girl who thrived,
but seal woman did not thrive.
Her skin grew dry, cracked, and white as the moon.
Her eyes grew dark as pebbles, her sight dimmed.
She never danced and her legs grew weak and thin.

At the seventh summer, in a voice of silver struck on stone,
seal woman cried, 'I want what I am made of returned to me.'
But the man refused. 'You would leave me wifeless,' he said.
Seal woman wept her weakness and despair,
and her daughter heard.
Loving her mother more than she feared to lose her,
she brought the skin that smelt of her mother's soul,
and her mother put it on. Seal woman kissed her daughter
          many times,
'I will always be with you, only touch what I have touched.'
Then she tore herself away, and disappeared beneath
          the waters.

Her daughter stayed because it was not her time
and on bright mornings she went down to the sea.
It was said she spoke to the seal whose skin
was like a salmon in springtime, and in time she became
a mighty drummer and singer and maker of stories.

So seal woman returned to her seal home—
as can all who've lost their skins
or had them taken from them.
The child is in you and there are many ways to return.

ALMOST
A WEEK

The first night without you,
I slept with the shanks of an old man
pressed up against me, loose flesh
and present sharply bone.

The second night without you,
I slept on the wide prairie.
How far I stretched my limbs
and met with no resistance,
a body shape in flattened wheat.

The third night without you,
I put on my black velvet dress,
played draughts with the proprietor
of a back street hotel. Ten games,
in exchange for the bed I slept in.

The fourth night without you,
I stayed awake, waiting for you,
but I was in a different city
and you could not find me.

The fifth night without you,
itinerant, I tied back my hair,
painted my face in its old colours,
slept with the window open
to let in the moths and the moon.

The sixth night without you,
a small creature, part swan,
part stone, part woman,
came and sat beside me,
sang me to sleep.

EASTER COTTAGE

Following a hand-drawn map
they find their next week's home
in turf sweet darkness,
four miles outside the village.
A place in nowhere,
a bubble in time,
someone else's life
they walk into, instantly
make their own.
Stones from the beach,
shells, a bird's skull, it is
as if they'd gathered them
themselves on winter walks.
Shelves of books
they'd always meant to read.
Comfortable in the deep dark
they love in Braille,
sleep as sound as the bodies
under the bog: their otherselves.

A TEMPORARY LEASE

I

Under Binevenagh and Eagle Hill,
in the Umbra, a thick green magic
veins the rock, runs through sap.

II

Across the railway tracks,
down a dark tunnel,
branches and brambles,
the hidden, rambling house.
Sunspotted, through leaves
of oak and beech.
Grown from one stone room,
earth floored, dark:

to a flowering of pantries,
bedrooms and bathrooms.
Then all the rest—
as each new generation
felt a need for more.
The last a ballroom,
parquet floored and huge,
French windows opening to air.

III

Tenanted there,
we dreamt a year—
tree green days
of talk and music.
Grass smoke nights
when we were satisfied.

Time changed to liquid,
so that we drifted
between centuries,
traversed lifetimes.
Back and forth so easily
we learnt to hear ghosts,
lived with their conversations.
Rhythms of dancing feet,
echoes of love in an empty room.

Each time we ventured out
the world was always further.

In that year we loved forever.

AFTER
THE
ARGUMENT...

we offer each other little treats.
Touch often, but with gentleness,
as if our skins might bruise
beneath the most delicate of caresses.
I bring flowers back into the house.
Vases full of heady honeysuckle,
minty hyssop. You cook omelettes
with brown eggs warm from straw:
we eat from the same plate.
Solicitous, we're careful in what we say,
for having thought ourselves immune
to chills, jealous fevers—it's shaken us.
We go to bed early on clean fresh sheets,
swear to take more care of ourselves.

OUT OF THE ORDINARY

Until now I had no faith to lose.
Then your belief taught me it is
ordinary things that speak the language
I once thought only God would use.
Chaos still rolls beyond our little fences,
and the wrong place is always only
a split second away. The cell can mutate,
brakes fail, and we must take our chances.

You hold off fear with small certainties,
and rhythmical days where each minute
flows easy to the next and into sleep.
Wakening with you I am at ease.
Few declarations, more steadfastness,
little considerations I so nearly missed.

HONEYMOON IN INDIA STREET

The knot tied, the present from her mother
spent on sparkling wine and sandwiches,
they took a black taxi home again.
Three hours did the round trip, with stops
at the City Hall, pub, off-licence.
There were no flowers.
While he lit the fire, she straightened
twisted sheets and tried to feel the difference,
went back downstairs to get another drink.

He offered her the glass with the worm in it.
'To my wife' the toast. She took and drank,
felt it slide down her contracting throat.
Gagged, but let it slip into her guts,
where it lay—foetal—while they made love.

VIRUS

'O Rose thou art Sick'
—William Blake

What's wrong between them is not obvious,
nothing acute, no open wound.
It's more like a virus they've both caught,
an undiagnosed syndrome
with peculiar clusters of symptoms.
Not yet understood, debilitating—
yet nothing to be done but wait it out
and see what happens.
Some might even say it was all in the mind.

She sits outside in the first rays of spring,
blanketed against the slight breeze.
Passing by, you would take her for an invalid,
convalescent, weak, her blood is tired, her heart,
and though the sun feels good, restorative,
she knows it will set too early.
Just before twilight she rises like an old woman,
goes back inside the house.

He has forgotten how to speak,
and the words he cannot use pile up,
begin to fester, reek of waste.
His flesh is overripe between his fingers
and awake when he should be asleep,
he feels himself ooze through the sheets
and down between the floorboards.
As he pours himself another drink,
he hears footsteps, and though he knows
she's there somewhere,
he cannot find her anywhere.

FLIRTATION

The sky is restless, sensual,
charged with a promise of thunder,

and he sparks with you, first glance.
He's witty, charming, funny,

live with the static of desire.
No touch entirely accidental,

and his words, rising into the dark
like fireflies, possibilities.

He meets your eyes, raises his glass
in an unspoken promise—passion,

new territories mapped on skin in truth—
but you hear the lie in it. Outside

the sky breaks to rain and you take
a taxi home to a warm domestic bed.

INFIDELITIES

After he'd gone,
she found money in the sheets,
fallen when he pulled his trousers off.
Gathering the coins into a small pile
she set them on the window ledge.
They sat, gathering dust, guilt,
until one day her husband
scooped them into his pocket.
Small change for a call
he couldn't make from the house.

POISONED GLEN

Hold your breath.
A woman could drown
in these dark loughs,
cold as forever.
Learn how to stop
at the surface,
see no deeper.
It is a kind of courage
to hear only what is said
—I love you—
balanced on liquid tension
like a pond skater.

Beneath, something almost seen,
a fin's flash in the dark weeds.

THE EMPEROR'S WIFE

She has become
as untrue as his stories,
insubstantial as his judgement.
As false as him.

All dressed up
in the fabric of his weaving,
she wonders why she feels so naked, so exposed.

LUNACY

for M.

Spring sharp, a full moon
sets the pillow to white flame,
burning her dark eyes.

She's plagued from sleep
by thoughts of him, splinters
under skin. Like today—

he lifted a stray thread
from her sleeve, with tenderness
it seemed, the way a lover might.

In truth, he remains alien as ever,
no closer to her knowing than if
their skins had never touched.

KISSING
GHOSTS

I'm as dark as the sky, tired as the year,
and it's a wet cold night: miserable.
All I really want is my seat by the fire,
T.V. turned on, mind turned off.
Instead, I'm driving in to town—

at the red light, my windscreen
blurs and clears
with the metronome of wipers,
so that every other second I see them.
Half inside a doorway,
half out in the rain,
kissing as if there were no weather.
He slips his hand inside her coat.
She tilts her hips towards him,
hand on the small of his back
pulling him closer.
Their eyes closed,
their mouths urgent.

In the crowded bar, a man
takes the seat beside me.
Fortyish and balding,
he sits down heavily,
stares at me.
'Moyra,' he says at last,
'it is, isn't it?' I'm suspicious,
I don't know this man,
his heavy Doric voice.
'Dave,' he persists,
'Don't you remember
the scooter ride we took?'
And from nowhere I do remember—
see him again.
A Scottish boy on a red Vespa.

He calls at my door, and I
hold him tight around the waist
as we take to the road together.

I search for a trace
of that boy I kissed
in the face of this intrusive stranger,
middle-aged and overweight.
He gives me a resumé
of his life to date.
His time in Stirling, his book,
the failed marriage,
a son he never sees.
He pauses, waits for me to speak,
and I oblige, reduce down
twenty years to five or six
brief sentences.

A silence grows.
He buys me a drink,
and, leaving, bends close
to touch his lips against my cheek.

EMMA, LEONARD AND GERMAINE

1970

I want to be Miss Peel,
brave and beautiful
in a white
bell-bottomed
trouser suit,
using lipstick
and intelligence
to find my way
out of the psychedelic maze
I've been lured into.
A mad scientist
has built a machine
to trap me,
drive me to suicide,
but I'm so cool
his plan just doesn't stand a chance
and I emerge unscathed,
my sexiness in place.
Even able
to make a joke at his expense.

1971

I paint my bedroom black,
hang out. Burning joss sticks
to cover the smell of the grass.
Ginsberg, Leary,
and the rest of the lads
have my head turned
with their non-sense
that seems to make more sense
than anything else.

Yeah man
—turn on, tune in and drop out—
dropping acid under the clock,
opening Mr. Huxley's doors.
Free love to Bowie and Reed,
—take a walk on the wild side.
Suicidal with Cohen.

1972
Ms. Greer strides
over my horizon, amazonian,
the flaming sword of truth in her hand.
I buy *Spare Rib*, go braless—
Liberation! Sisterhood!

1973
I'm existentialist.

DRIVING BACK ALONE FROM MAYO

No need for signposts
in a country crisscrossed
with trails of other journeys,
winter sun at my back
pushing me east.
I bless each familiar thing
and set my mind on constancy,
telling myself stories we could become,
re-inventing our history.
I was faithful, content,
love made you articulate.
The fiction of what should have been
is a map unfolding, a way home.

STUDENTS
IN
ATHENS

In a cool square, out of the main city swelter,
beneath the shade of an olive tree,
a young man leans back in his chair.
He drains his cup of thick dark coffee,
then lights a cigarette. He is content as a cat.
The young woman with him raises a camera.

A year from now, when they are no longer lovers,
she will think of that momentary eternity,
the leaves of the olive tree dripping shadows
across the white tablecloth, the secret knowledge
of her body, touched only by him and the sun.
Bitter and sweet.

Twenty years from now, she'll come across
the photograph at the back of a drawer
and be taken back at how young they were.
She'll feel a restlessness and wonder
whatever became of them.

TRABANE

I weave this summer's time
on memory's frame.
Weft of air, warp of water
catching all the light.
Azure meeting of sky and lake,
red pools of sun's sinking.
I hold every colour, lichened boulders,
sea shades and coral strands,
where children touched with gold
climb rocks for starfish, shrimps.
Among the purple-brown Twelve Bens
I weave our love's calm colours
through passion's bright threads—
sleep beautiful. Winter,
I'll throw this cloth across our bed.

THE
LAST
SUMMER

for Joan Newmann

The dulse they picked is drying in the sun,
white with sea salt, sharp to taste.
Little flat fish wriggle beneath her toes.
Daddy holds her hand against the waves,
while mummy watches from a deck chair
on the sand. Faces smiling: her family.
Then quietly, nights closed in,
and Autumn returned them home.

Pots they stacked, neat in rows,
grass mowings, language beneath.
In long shadow, behind the hedge,
her uncle gardens betrayal, an adult pain.
She becomes an initiate in silence.
As grown up secrets seed
Daddy lets go of her hand,
Mummy doesn't see her anymore,
and she learns how to pretend,
becomes one of the family.

The shutter closes, takes and holds
always their faces: always the pose.

CATCHING THE LIVERPOOL BOAT

for S.

You were the girl!
Free from family
and small town eyes,
you hit the city.
Parties, pints
in the Club Bar
where you could pull
any man you wanted–
and why not?
Sauce for the gander
and all that.
Many's the one
was set on fire
by the bright flame
of your hair.

No big deal
you said,
but when you came back,
you scissored your hair
to a pool on the floor,
swirling about your feet
bright as fresh blood.

SHE
DREAMS...

The young man is peeling her an orange
while a foreign sun ripens outside the window.
His fingers, juicy, separate each segment carefully.
She is calm, knowing he will simply place the fruit
on a white plate and offer it to her.
She is not his wife or mother,
or anything she doesn't know how to be.
He is not her lover, though she knows
how his skin would taste.
The orange is sweet, the room is quiet.
No one speaks her name.

The young man has made her a poem
by erasing words, lines, even whole stanzas.
As he hands her the page, clean and white,
the final metaphor flutters to the floor.
She has no fear, knowing he will leave it unsaid—
there is no question, no rhyme or reasoning.
Even his eyes say nothing.

HEARTS

All day he works with hearts,
to understand them better.
Know how this muscle pumps,
contracts to its function.
In his palm, the rabbit's heart
still flutters, as he injects
the enzymes, breaks it down.

Brought to its single self
under the microscope, each cell
reveals to him its nature,
gives measured answers.
Chromatographic shades of meaning
extracted, written down, definitive.

At night, he lays his head
on the soft billow of her breast:
hears the measuring of time, and all
heart's anarchies beat in his ear.

THE APOTHECARY

for John

He understands the garden, works
with its seasons. Nothing lies fallow.
Hedges protect, shelter new green,
sap runs to the core, brilliant,
so the earth does not smell of decay.
He has planted herbs for healing,
nothing grows in vain. Even names
become a litany against dis-ease,
sweet and musical upon her tongue.
Comfrey, Feverfew, Valerian,
Amara Dulcis, Angelica, Golden Thyme.
Seeds of peony in wine to cure the nightmare,
Oil of Cowslip to assuage the forgetful evil.
By old remedies and the art of ordinary means,
patiently, he conducts her to health.
Blue stars of Borage to gladden her heart,
Eyebright, so she can see the colours of his love.
He has made an apothecary's den,
where bees drink from honeyed cups
and small birds tumble branch to branch.
Distillations of scent and sound
lift on the morning air to her bedroom window,
dreams of lushness, fragrant awakening.

MOUNTAIN GROWN

On the darkest winter day of the year,
he produces his stash of last summer's pressed heads,
and into our lungs we suck the strength of rock,
juice of earth, liquid sun and song of birds.
Hold—Exhale.
Feel the mountain's wild heart.

SLIEVE LEAGUE

I stand on mica, quartz,
breathe the far view,
taste the dizzying depths,
salt on my tongue.
Waves' deep detonations
echo down chambers of my ears:
the land's heartbeat.
Out to sea, huge tracts of water move,
green swallows blue.

This place knows nothing of me.
Unlike the delicate flowers, the sheep
and gulls who live here, I have no part.
Tomorrow I am gone.
These sounds, this thin air,
this savage grace remains.
I lean on the wind's indifference.

OUTSIDE
IS
BREAKING
IN

Creepers and stalkers, the plants finger my sill
like burglars, waiting only
the opportunity of my carelessness,
a window left open overnight.
Doors leak dust and with every rain
damp flowers across my bedroom wall,
osmosis through brick, blisters in paint.
The wind pushes small feathers and wisps
of straw through the letter box,
and tiny claws of mice pattern
my thoughts with their comings and goings.
Midges drown themselves in my wine,
daddy-long-legs hide in the sink,
or blunder about without looking
and heavy metallic-blue flies
hang in the air like thugs,
buzzing with ignorant purpose.
Slugs congregate when I am sleeping,
leave trails of mocking silver evidence
across the kitchen floor.
Tonight a bat circles the light,
hallucinatory black, like a negative,
then settles on the curtains.

CLAIRE AND THE MOON

Tonight the moon hung low, full,
bloated with summer.
Feeling its pull we went outside,
where silver half-light
showed the familiar strange.
Pipistrelles swooped to feed, calling.
I was too old to hear them
but they spoke for you.
Fat hens shuffled on their perches,
uneasy, as across the field
a dog fox looked for shadow.

Suddenly, letting go of my hand,
you raised your arms to the sky
and danced: a small dance
there on the shining grass—
your partner the moon, no part for me.

CARVING
AT
NEWGRANGE

Aboriginal, I belong to every mouth.
My origins sacred and human, are older
than the batholith from which I was chiselled.

I am written in stone, a language all verb,
remembered in the meiosis of cells,
and understood with heart not head.

KOBI

a found poem

We were making the final preparations
for the New Year Tea Ceremony,
when the earth leapt up with a sound like doom.
We have a saying—
if a thing happens twice, it will happen again.

MOTHS

Colour of Miss Havisham's dress,
their lace wings, frantic,
smear my window with distress.
The soft thuds of their bodies on the glass,
their frail persistence, sickens me.
I can see no virtue in this fragility,
this futile burning for the light. No need.
I can blow out the flame, release us into the dark.

MAKE HAY

Summer fades from skin
and the pull begins, down.
Limbs grow heavy, light leaves
through the top of my head.

Outside, colours grow colder.

I find myself loitering outside florists
among buckets of bright flowers,
jittery as a user who needs to score.
On my back, the monkey of winter.

DREAMING
HOUSES

First is a bungalow,
all fifties lines, bay windows,
and a small front garden,
a gate right out onto the beach.
On the steep hill behind
a black horse gallops ceaselessly round
and round in sweat, caught
on a constant carousel.
Only its eyes remain untamed, its teeth bared.
Inside I am constrained to one small room,
the larger comfort and the view of sea
forbidden to me. I can only stand at the door
and hope that someday I'll be allowed in there.

Second is seventeenth century,
long corridors, high ceilings
and many hidden rooms,
priest holes, full of the dark.
Through Claude's black convex glass
the landscape is diminished, despite
its perfected winding river,
distant hills, glimpse of the sea.
This place is everywhere to me, so
I am content, knowing no better,
besides, sometimes I am allowed
to walk for a while with my friend.
We stroll through formal gardens,
between geometric lines of hedges and borders,
talking a little, before she has to leave again.

Third is mud and wattle,
snail shaped, whorl upon whorl I follow,
round and down to the deep centre.
Here and there the roof has fallen in,
opening the sky, but mostly
it is mole dark and burrow safe.

The fourth is built on rock
metamorphic,
its walls are infinite
and I am roofed in light.

A Note from the Publisher

CavanKerry Press regularly reserves a place on its calendar for publishing out-of-print books that deserve permanence. Bringing *lost* books back to life is core to the CavanKerry ethos and in this way, we honor the work of the writer.

Joan Cusack Handler